In My Mind

Judith Olivas

BookLeaf Publishing

India | USA | UK

Presentation by *BookLeaf Publishing*

Web: www.bookleafpub.com

E-mail: info@bookleafpub.com

ISBN: 9789360945381

First edition 2024

I want to dedicate this book to my family, especially my parents. Thank you, dad, for always providing for us and thank you, mom, for pushing me to get published before I finished high school.

I also want to dedicate this book to all the English teachers I've had over the years. Thank you for being amazing educators and for encouraging my love of writing.

PREFACE

I always liked writing. Mostly because I liked reading. In second grade, I joined a creative writing club and started jotting down short stories. From that moment on, my goal was to become an author/illustrator by combining my two favorite things, writing and drawing.

I joined band in 5th grade and began playing trombone. It quickly took over my attention (I love it) and I started to wonder if writing was really what I wanted to do for the rest of my life. As I got older, I discovered my passion lay in music and leadership, prompting me to become a music educator.

I'm extremely satisfied with this career pathway, but I couldn't help but think about the little girl that had her heart set on being an author. The little girl with a mind full of stories that she wanted to share with the world. I excelled in music, but she always stayed in the back of my mind.

I realized, one day, why should I have to give up one dream for another? Why not have both?

Being able to complete these poems and get them published is one of my favorite accomplishments. It honors not only those that shaped my life, but also the little girl with dreams bigger than herself. It serves as a vow that I will follow my passions and interests and keep listening to my heart.

North Loop

White pillars with scattered dandelions at their
base
In the grass where I looked for bugs and rocks
A long field with sixteen trees with pecans
Small apricots the birds would beat us to
Fruit eaten, scattered in the ditch
A winding vine grew grapes with tough skin
I love the sun through the branches
I loved being one with you
Make me one with you forever
Turn my veins into roots and plant me
Make my eyes glisten in the sun

Pottery

I crouched at the bank of the ditch
And dug my fingers into the muddy clay
I grabbed a stick
And sculpted with my stubby fingers
I mushed and pulled and prodded
Until a vase formed in my palms
I picked a flower for it
And gifted it to the woman inside

Nap

3

I was probably no more than 4
Staring down sopita in a bowl
Now it was empty
And my stomach was full
I fell asleep
Tough day at pre-k
I guess
I half-awoke to her voice asking him to carry me
Strong arms lifted me from my chair at the table
Carried me to the bedroom
And tucked me in

Tamales

The kitchen smelled like vitamins and masa
I climbed onto the chair at the head of the table
And rested on my knees
I was handed a bowl and taught how to knead
I inspected every spec of corn that passed
through my fingers
And watched my dad and grandmother smooth
the mixture
In corn husks that were then placed in a pot.
When I got to try one, cooked,
It didn't taste how I thought
But I was too overwhelmed by my pride
That I had helped make them
That I barely noticed

Wish You Were Here

I didn't believe you left
It was just entirely too quick
Sometimes I forget and I catch myself
Thinking of future memories we's make
And then I remember.
I miss you
I think of you often
I hope, wherever you are, you think of me too

Rainy Day

The clouds roll in quietly
And despite the lack of sun, the afternoon stays
warm
If I have a chance, maybe I'll slip out to the
backyard
Take in the breeze and let the air breathe life into
my lungs
Droplets of water make polka dots on the ground
And as the downpour increases its pitter patter
A shiver runs down my spine
So I go inside before I get told
That if I stay outside too long I'll catch a cold

Clouds

7

What's it like to be a cloud?
I wonder.
To be so high up
To be passed through by planes and bird that
dare to fly high enough
If I were a cloud I'd make shapes out of myself
For the little people below to look up and point
And marvel at the coincidences of nature

Adventure

8

The smell of diesel and gasoline and exhaust
I breathe it in
I savor
The sensation brings back memories
Of bus rides
Of truck stops
Of travels to somewhere, to do something fun
I let it settle in
Before we have to leave, off to the next
destination

Balloon Fiesta and Donut Holes

We brought lawn chairs
And set them on the grass
Oh, we were freezing
Blankets upon blankets were layered
But we stayed shivering
Until
Fire!
Small fires, everywhere
Lit under giant, colorful balloons
And as they rose, the people in their baskets
grew tiny
And we watched, amazed
Forgetting how cold we were

Section Leader Duties

They asked me to get to practice early, and I
groaned
I dragged myself out of bed an hour early
And helped them pull podiums from storage
We'd prop them on our shoulders
And roll them to the stadium for Friday's
practice
Setting up was always over sooner than I
thought
And on the walk back to the school from the
field
I'd look up at the stars
And trace out the patterns I knew

A Belt of Stars

The moon is high
I raise my head
The stars
The guides
I search for the familiar patterns until I find him
I know where he is
Three stars in a line
Orion, my friend
Always watching, silent
You've seen me every day, looking up at you
What is the view from up there?
What do you see?

Friday Night Lights

The sun was too hot and bright
Isn't that how its ought to be?
My uniform is snug around my body
The chill of a water bottle seeps through my
gloves
Clang of metal
My instrument set down
A faint smell of hamburgers floats up
"I wish those were for us"
"Mm hm"
We sit
And wait eagerly for halftime
The sun begins to sink, savoring its last
moments

Last Lap

I hit every note
I smiled like I had never smiled before
Life was breathed into my movements
And when the performance was done
I ran
Full force, hair billowing
To the back of the field
To my family on the track
Away from my family in the stands
Sweet tears spilled down my face
I mourned those that couldn't be there in that
moment
And I wanted to cherish everyone that was
Does it get better than this?

Danzon

I want to perform concerts for the rest of my life
I want to sit
Or stand
On a stage
With many other musicians
I want to make music
And I want it to be fun
I want the lights to blind me
And I want cheers from the audience to deafen
me
You can take those senses from me
I just want to feel the music

Flashback

I thought flashbacks weren't real
I thought they were the kind of thing
Only seen in movies and books
But then all of a sudden i was a little girl
Who didn't know how to tie her shoes
Walking outside shops in San Antonio
And when I came back to the present
I was suddenly 18
My feet were in the same place as they were
back then
And although my life had changed drastically
since
I felt the same

A Burst of Creativity

A line there
Maybe a few squiggles here
Hm.
Stray ink marks dance on my hands.
Make a circle here.
That doesn't look right
Erase
Try again
It needs color.
How do I?
There's too many choices
That's what makes it fun

The Garden of Artistry

17

Why do artists paint fruits?
Is it simply the variety?
How the carefully placed seeds on a strawberry
Contrast the gentle curve of a banana
Or the pearl-ish nature of a grape?
Or are they painted for the novelty
Knowing fruit has touched the lips of every
human
Since the beginning of time?

Reflection

When I look in the mirror
I study
The shape of my face
The bridge of my nose and dip of my lips
How many others before me
Have shared these same features?
I wish I knew all the stories
Of the people that fell in love
And gave their faces to their children
Who would then give them to me

Lucky

What are the odds our souls were placed
So specifically
That we'd have such an imprint on each other's
hearts
I wouldn't be who I am without you
Bits of everyone became parts of me
And every night
Before I drift off
I think of how grateful I am
To love others that love me right back

To Be Alive

When the room is quiet
And I have nothing to do
I lay down and listen
I hear my breath
And I feel the strong thump of my heart
As it hammers in my chest
To become keenly aware of your body
Is to be keenly aware of your soul
And I'm amused at the miracle of our existence

I Hope

When I have lived my life
And done everything I was meant to do
I hope I am happy
I hope I remember who I was
And who I still am
And the people that got me to where I ended up
I hope my life is colorful
And when I cross the barrier between this world
and the next
I hope I am not regretful

www.ingramcontent.com/pod-product-compliance
Lightning Source LLC
Chambersburg PA
CBHW071249140726
47996CB00007B/2815